CATHARS, WHITE EAGLE AND ST JOHN

COLUM HAYWARD

Cathars, White Eagle and St John

Articles and Talks

Polair
Publishing

POLAIR PUBLISHING

KENSINGTON · LONDON
www.polairpublishing.co.uk

First published January 2015
in a limited edition of 150 copies
by Polair Publishing, 295 Ladbroke Grove,
London W10 6HE

No. 119 of 150 copies

British Library Cataloguing in Publication Data
A catalogue record for this book is available
from the British Library

ISBN 978-1-905398-32-4

Set in Joanna by the Publisher and printed in
the United Kingdom by Lightning Source

Contents

Acknowledgments

I am grateful to Jenny Dent and the White Eagle Publishing Trust for permission to reprint the ten articles from the magazine *Stella Polaris* that appeared under the title 'The White Eagle Cathar' from 2013.

I am also grateful to Jenny and her family for hospitality in Yorkshire over Christmas 2014, during which time this book began to be put together, and to Charlotte Lochhead for loan of her cottage in Dorchester, Oxon., where the book was completed.

Colum Hayward
London, 2014

Introduction

This book reproduces one talk and ten short articles, each of them given in a context of the White Eagle Lodge membership, and adds an epilogue. I hope that the whole will have a relevance to readers outside White Eagle Lodge too, and that such readers will simply find that White Eagle's teaching informs and helps in the development of an understanding of what it felt like, spiritually, to be a Cathar, which is what it is most difficult to appreciate from the histories.

Of course, to be Cathar was also to be possessed of the mediaeval mind, and that we cannot expect of ourselves. However, there is an underlying assumption in the book that there is a state of consciousness we can achieve that is not of the ordinary mind, and not fettered by time and place, but the kind of awareness we know in meditation, and that in this consciousness we might be 'Cathar' without being 'mediaeval'. Such awareness will be held only at a particular level, but it may be helpful to explore it. It is because he helps us develop this sort of consciousness that White Eagle's teaching is helpful to the student. Since the term 'Cathar' was quite foreign to those who were labelled 'Cathar', the use of it to imply some sort of spiritual viewpoint independent of time and place seems at the least no more paradoxical than to use it of thirteenth-century believers.

The first, and longest, piece of writing was given as a talk on the occasion of the launch of Polair Publishing's title, THE CATHAR VIEW, in 2012. THE CATHAR VIEW (edited by Dave Patrick)* is a series of essays by all sorts of writers, some of whom would be the first to acknowledge that they are primitive in their scholarly understanding of the Cathars and some who are by contrast relatively learned. One proposition of the book is that Catharism, whatever it is, is available to all who aspire to understand it. I contributed two chapters to that volume, which may be read alongside what is here. One of them is entitled 'Cathar Joy', while the other describes 'A Trip to the Ariège in 1931'. The latter relates to a visit made by my grandmother, Grace Cooke, which

*London, Polair Publishing, 2012

is important to the present book and to my own study of the Cathars. She was taken there, with her husband Ivan, by the French Polaire brothers, who were themselves pioneers of Cathar study. Among them I honour in this book both Maurice Magre and the controversial, but maybe misunderstood, Otto Rahn.

White Eagle also sent a young student named Walter Birks to the Languedoc to pursue investigations and understand Cathar beliefs; he turned strongly against his early teachers but his conclusions, published much later, nonetheless inform some of the articles in this book.*

The rest of the book, apart from an Epilogue I have added, is a set of ten articles that has been appearing in the bi-monthly White Eagle magazine *Stella Polaris* since August 2013, excepting August 2014, under the title 'The White Eagle

*Walter Birks and R. A. Gilbert, THE TREASURE OF MONTSÉGUR. Wellingborough, Northants., Aquarian Press, 1990. Otto Rahn's most notable book was CRUSADE AGAINST THE GRAIL, published in German in 1933 but not translated into English until 2006 (Rochester, VT, Bear & Co.). The work by Maurice Magre that is of greatest interest to us was THE RETURN OF THE MAGI, published in English in 1931 but in French, as MAGICIENS ET ILLUMINÉS, in 1930.

Cathar'. Here, I have given them titles of their own. White Eagle has spoken over such a long period of the likelihood of White Eagle brethren having lived before, in Cathar times, that it seemed important to flesh out this connection for a White Eagle readership.

Reincarnation, so much a feature of Arthur Guirdham's Cathar studies,* doesn't get mentioned very much in the articles, but it is there, in the Cathar belief that only going through the ceremony of rebirth into a supernal understanding could free the human consciousness, otherwise held by matter or darkness. There are other subjects the articles scarcely mention, for they are selective in their scope: the Cathar dietary constraints, for instance (largely vegan but permitting fish), the promise of the Cathar to travel in pairs, like the first apostles, and the absolute commitment to being truthful that made them such innocent victims of the Inquisition. Tied to truthfulness but not to giving away their companions' names, they took upon themselves the price of such commitment.

*Beginning with THE CATHARS AND REINCARNATION (London, 1970)

Some themes, of course, are repeated. That is the nature of this book – a collection of separate pieces of writing. One day, soon, I hope there will be a consistent book to follow it, explaining how we can be Cathars (in the sense I have described) today, if we espouse a certain inner awareness of the light and live from it. To some extent this book is a taster. The articles in *Stella Polaris* sometimes referred to White Eagle teachings printed in the same issue of the magazine, and I have done my best to put these together in an appendix. I have edited the articles only slightly for inclusion here, adding a few explanatory footnotes. I begin with a brief chronology, for readers with a relatively misty awareness of historical dates.

There is an occasion for this book's publication, which is an event offered at the Questhaven Retreat near San Diego, California, which was shared by followers of the teacher Flower A. Newhouse and by White Eagle members in California. For that reason I dedicate it not only to my many White Eagle friends but to the followers of Flower Newhouse, also.

A Cathar Chronology

The dates below describe not only events directly involving Cathars, but relevant 'external' events too (italicized in the list). The Bogomils in Bulgaria held similar beliefs but within the Eastern church; the Waldensians were another group who chose a purist form of Christianity over the Church's offering, and the Templars, originally those who accompanied and formed a support network for the Crusaders in the Holy Land, and whose foundation was thus very different, nonetheless came to be persecuted in the wake of the Cathar persecution. The reforms of Pope Gregory, which begin the list, were intended to root out the very abuses in the Church that the Cathars so strongly rejected.

1050   Reforms of Gregory the Great begin
1085   Many Bogomils imprisoned in Bulgaria
1100   Unmasking of Basil, a leading Bogomil teacher
1101   Persecution begins of Waldensian sect ('Poor

Men of Lyons')

1129	Templars endorsed by Catholic church
1143	First possible mention of Cathar-like heresy, in Cologne
1147	Papal legate sent to arrest progress of Cathars
1160	Attack on the Cathar heresy by Hildegard of Bingen
1180	First armed expedition against the Cathars by Henry of Marcy
1181/2	Birth of Francis of Assisi
1198	Innocent III crowned; begins organized suppression of Cathar heresy
1203	Dominic de Guzman (later St Dominic) debates with Cathars
1206	Programme of conversion and debate by Diego of Osma and his canon, Dominic
1208	Excommunication of Raymond VI of Toulouse by papal legate Pierre de Castelnau, who is subsequently murdered
1209	Launch of crusade against the Cathars
	Siege of Béziers, with enormous loss of life, maybe 20,000
	Simon de Montfort given command of crusader army after
1213	Battle of Muret, at which Philip II of Aragon,

who defends Cathars, is killed

1215 Fourth Council of the Lateran

1216 Dominican order established

1218 Death of de Montfort at siege of Toulouse

1226 Death of Francis of Assisi

1229 Treaty of Paris ends crusade with King of France dispossessing the house of Toulouse and the Viscounts of Béziers and Carcassonne

1234 Inquisition begins; continues throughout thirteenth and much of fourteenth century

1244 Massacre at Montségur

1255 Fall of Quéribus; Cathars hiding there escape to Aragon or Piedmont

1295/6 Authié brothers visit Piedmont and revive Catharism in Ariège

1307 Persecution begins of Knights Templar

1310 Cathar revival suppressed with execution of Pierre Authié in Toulouse

1321 Last known Cathar *parfait*, Guillaume Bélibaste, executed

1330 Very little mention of Cathars in Inquisition records from this time on

St John – the First Cathar?

A talk given at the White Eagle Lodge, St Mary Abbots Place, London W8, on 20 October 2012, the occasion of the launch of the book THE CATHAR VIEW*

I WANT to begin this talk at a very personal level. In July 1931 my grandmother, Grace Cooke, five years before she founded the White Eagle Lodge, made a trip to the south of France and stayed in a hotel at Ax-les-Thermes, in the valley of the River Ariège. It was a highly unusual trip for an English person, and it was specifically intended by those with whom she was working that it would bring her into contact with whatever remained of the mediaeval Albigenses or Cathars, and maybe even help them find a treasure that was secreted there. In the 1930s the subject of the Cathars was coming into vogue in France, but had hardly reached England at all.

The particular site under investigation was not Montségur but one of the smaller Cathar

*See p. 8

castles or châteaux, that of Lordat, slightly north of Ax and perched high above the valley. With Grace Cooke went Ivan, her husband, who was also possessed of mediumistic gifts, although – he would have been the first to insist – to a lesser degree than she. Also present was Zam Bhotiva, author of the French original of the second book we are launching today, ASIA MYSTERIOSA,* and one of the Cookes' hosts. His book describes the wisdom-source of a group of which he was co-founder, which called itself in French 'Le Groupe des Polaires'. There was also present a mutual friend, Mrs Betty Caird Miller. 'A Visit to Ariège in 1931' is the title of one of the chapters I have contributed to the book which is our principal launch this afternoon, THE CATHAR VIEW.

During this trip, my grandmother (I shall henceforth call her Grace Cooke) unexpectedly had a vision – a vision so powerful that, as she later remembered, it left her in a daze of happiness for weeks after. It had a huge impact on our work

*Zam Bhotiva, ASIA MYSTERIOSA : THE ORACLE OF ASTRAL FORCE AS A MEANS OF COMMUNICATION WITH 'THE LITTLE LIGHTS OF THE ORIENT'. Paris, 1929; English translation, with a preface by Colum Hayward, October 2012

in the White Eagle Lodge; indeed, we might quite reasonably claim that the origin of the Lodge lies in this trip, and in this vision. Let me quote from Grace Cooke's own account of it, given in the foreword to THE LIVING WORD (1949; 1979, as THE LIVING WORD OF ST JOHN), a compilation of White Eagle's teaching around the gospel of St John. Therein, looking back some eighteen years, she describes how, gazing out across the mountains that form a backdrop to Lordat and extend into the main chain of the Pyrenees, 'my attention was caught by the sudden appearance of a shining form'.

'Shining' was a strong word in her vocabulary; she had earlier described the special presence of her guide White Eagle as 'the Shining Presence'.* I am not sure how physical the shining being felt to her: she knew he was not of this earth, but describes him as though what she saw had taken a very earthly form:

'His manner was as normal as that of any human being might be who, while out walking, had stumbled by chance upon a stranger. He appeared simply, kindly, and treated the situation

*The title of her book containing memoirs of two sequential lives, published in 1946

— 17 —

as naturally as if it were customary for discarnate people to talk to men and women. He looked like an old man at first sight; that is to say, he wore a longish white beard and his hair was silver, but apart from this his skin was youthful and clear, as though a light shone behind the flesh, and his warm blue eyes were alight with an inner fire. He was clothed in white, in the garb of some early order of Christian Brothers, and bore himself with noble meekness.'

The signs that this being then gave convinced her that he was one of the so-called Cathars who had peopled these hills and valleys six or seven centuries before. She wondered – as we human beings do – if he had perhaps come to help the little party (which by now included a small contingent from France itself) to tyffind the legendary treasure. He assured her that treasure existed, but before it was found, lessons had to be learnt by humanity. Until then it would be well-guarded and hidden, lest it be misused. What was required first was a development of a special sort of moral wisdom, which he called 'soul-knowledge':

'Only through development of this soul-knowledge and its use for the good of all, would humanity qualify to find the buried treasure. For the spiritual law is that the candidate for initiation into the mysteries of life, both human and spiritual, must proceed on his course without deviation, patiently and steadfastly discovering and uncovering within his own divine nature attributes and powers which will give him the key to wealth, both physical and spiritual. Therefore it seemed that the first step towards the locating of this treasure was to find some spiritual clue which would help us towards the completion of our task.'

But there was more to the message, and it is what most affects us in view of the title of our talk today. She writes,

'In the life and teaching of Jesus the Christ, our visitor continued, would be found the key to the spiritual treasure buried within man. After the resurrection and departure of his Master one of his disciples, John the beloved, had voyaged to the west and had visited this same mountain, where he had spent long hours in spiritual communion with his Master. Then, returning to the east, John had founded the Brotherhood (which became known as the Albigenses), imparting to it the wisdom that he had learnt from his Master. Its treasure and its secret was that store of spiritual wisdom which might indeed be called the complete gospel of St John, of which the existing gospel is but a fragment. Before his passing John had been called to the Sages in the east, where he had spent the last years of his life. Nor did John die as most men die, but passed onwards to the higher life as his Master had done before him.

'Many centuries later it appears that the Brotherhood founded by John took ship and sailed to the west, subsequently settling among the mountains of France, where they became known as the Albigenses. They were in fact still the Brethren of John, the founder of their group, whose gospel was their secret and their treasure.'

Well, that is the story with which we may begin. It is not a conventional story. No surviving manuscript documents John's visit to the west. Many more people today promote the story of the conversion of an area of Provence and beyond by Mary Magdalene than ever mention John. I am not, on what we know today, going to be able to prove or disprove the point made by the mystical figure in the vision.

Let's look at a few issues, though. The first is that one thing every Cathar seems to have been certain of was that the tradition they upheld was in direct lineage with the early Church and was the untarnished truth, the authentic Christianity. Cathars never called themselves Cathars or even Albigeois: those are the names history (mainly written by their persecutors) has given them. All they ever called themselves was 'good Christians', and the local people, who appreciated the care shown by these simple beings, called them 'bonshommes' and 'bonnes femmes', the good men and women. Among the gospels, John's was pre-eminent to them.

Modern scholarship, which was way beyond Grace Cooke's reach, has shown how the rituals of Catharism — the consolamentum ceremony in particular — go back to the 'Love Feast' or agape of the early Church. It resembles that primitive ceremony more than the Mass does, and the Cathars rejected the doctrine of the transubstantiation. One modern authority, Walter Birks, has also suggested that a forgotten sect in Syria, notionally Muslim but strangely Christian in its ceremonies, holds another key to the traditions the Cathars took directly from early Christianity. It was the belief that the individual life is there to be filled with light, exactly like the filling of the grail cup. Each man and woman is a 'cup in which God can be made manifest'.*

There has now been quite a long tradition of writers who have connected the Cathars with the custodianship of the Holy Grail, but not as long a custodianship as the one Birks put forward. Really to understand why the image connects with the Cathars at all we need to turn to St John's gospel – the fourteenth chapter – which although it does not seem to have been read in full in the consolation ceremony, nonetheless supplies us with the primary locus for that word 'consolation' in any Christian worship.

'If ye love me, keep my commandments. And I will pray the Father, and he shall give you another Comforter, that he may abide with you for ever: even the spirit of truth, whom the world cannot receive, because it seeth him not: but ye know him, for he dwells with you, and shall be in you. I will not leave you comfortless: I will come to you.

'Yet a little while, and the world seeth me no more; but

*For Birks' book, see p. 9. The crucial chapter appears also in THE CATHAR VIEW, and the reference there is p. 195.

ye see me: because I live, ye shall live also. At that day ye shall know that I am in my Father, and ye in me, and I in you.'

(John 14 : 15–20)

If that tells us distinctly more about the word 'Comforter' — which has effectively the same meaning as 'Consoler' — there is more to come.

'If a man love me, he will keep my words: and my Father will love him, and we will come unto him, and make our abode with him. He that loveth me not keepeth not my sayings: and the word which ye hear is not mine, but the Father's which sent me. These things have I spoken unto you, being yet present with you. But the Comforter, which is the Holy Ghost, whom that Father will send in my name, he shall teach you all things, and bring all things to your remembrance, whatsoever I have said unto you.'

(John 14 : 23–26)

The Comforter, then, is indeed the Holy Ghost, perhaps seen by the Cathars in some special way that precedes the doctrine of the Trinity, which was established relatively late in the early Church. But in this identification with the presence also known as the Holy Breath, I think we have the key both to the ritual of consolamentum — the coming or breathing in of the Comforter — and of the presence of God actually in our own being.

'I am in my Father, and ye in me, and I in you.' (v. 20): an exquisite three-way interpenetration indeed! The realized knowledge of this unity, I believe, is precisely what the Cathars had and felt they could not give away, ever – to a church who postponed salvation to some remote after-death day of judgment. It was a sense of mystical revelation – the Gnostic element in Catharism, if you like – by which the presence of the subjective 'I' within God was absolutely real; the presence of God within the subjective 'I' was also real; and heaven, the world of light, the way that Jesus showed, was an experience that could be had now, in this minute.

It was a revelation that could hold you transfixed – transfigured, even, in that your whole being changed with it – until such time as death took you – and a violent, early death, such as burning, might hold no horrors at all. Is it sheer coincidence that the Pic de St-Barthélémy, the mountain that rises up behind Lordat and separates it from Montségur – the one that the vision speaks of, we assume – is known locally by the name 'Montagne de Tabe', apparently a corruption of the biblical name, Mount Tabor? Mt Tabor was the mountain upon which the Transfiguration is said to have taken place. And so to the Cathar to be 'consoled' was to manifest the Holy Spirit, because you were a transfigured being of light, quite unaffected by the darkness of the earth.

Here is Walter Birks again.

'The good man was once more an angel and as such an object of veneration to his fellow-men, among whom he moved like another Christ. But if he had achieved the privileges of Christhood he had also incurred the obligation to live like Christ and to devote himself entirely to the salvation of his fellows still in [earth's] prison. His renunciation of the world must be entire.' (THE TREASURE OF MONTSÉGUR, p. 84)

It is very easy for scholars to see the Cathars in a very this-world kind of a way; to recognize their dualism, the belief that the earth was darkness until you manifested the light — and yet to fail to recognize that Cathars lived and suffered for something. The understanding of the experience that something was, I should like to suggest, is to be found in St John's gospel, here and in many other passages.

And we know that St John's gospel was

everything to the Cathars. Unlike Catholics, they carried this specific gospel with them, even in the vernacular: maybe in a complete New Testament, but frequently as a single item. To be found carrying St John's gospel on its own was enough to bring you before the Inquisition. There were favourite Cathar texts in the other gospels, and in the epistles of both Paul and John, but nothing else held quite the appeal of John's gospel. Did not the very basis of dualism, war between light and dark, lie in words such as *And the light shineth in the darkness, and the darkness comprehended it not* (John 1 : 5)? All the first seventeen verses of St John, the part known as the Prologue or Prolegomena, formed part of the *consolamentum* liturgy.

We may therefore ask whether Cathars had access to works associated with John outside of the scriptural Canon. Well, definitely 'yes' to one such work. It is known variously as the 'Book of John', the *Interrogio Johannis*, or 'The Secret Supper', and in translation from the Latin it begins with the sentence 'The questions of John, the apostle and evangelist, at a secret supper in the kingdom of heaven, about the governance of this world, about its ruler, and about Adam'. It is a work describing a cosmology somewhat alien to our pattern of thinking today: the fall of the rebel angels, and the position of the human being (represented by Adam and Eve) finely poised between the two worlds. It describes the seven ages for which Satan will rule over the earth, and the final restitution of divine power: the rule of the angels, culminating in phrases that marry with the biblical Revelation of St John:

'And God shall be in their midst. "They shall no more hunger nor thirst, neither shall the sun fall on them nor any heat. And God shall wipe away every tear from their eyes." And he shall reign with his Holy Father, and his reign shall endure forevermore.'

(Printed in Walter L. Wakefield and Austin P. Evans, HERESIES OF THE HIGH MIDDLE AGES. New York (Columbia), 1991; compare Revelation 7 : 17)

It is easy for us to become so immersed in St John's gospel, we forget this other world, the world of Revelation. But it is assumed by scholars that the Book of John or Secret Supper, though it may go back to some very early Gnostic text, was something progressively transformed over the centuries, for it contains some hints that its original language was Slavonic or Greek, and one of the two versions we have is known to have come from Bulgaria. It may belong, primarily to the Bulgarian Bogomils. The other copy is from Inquisition archives in Carcassonne.

Another apocryphal Johannine text with a Gnostic source, this time believed to be as old as the second century, is known as the 'Acts of John'. It survives only in fragments and as far as I know it is not possible to show that it was available to the Cathars. On the other hand, if they were as firmly in the Johannine tradition as seems to be the case, even if they did not have the full text, there may have been elements of it carried down orally in the tradition. We only have fragments of it today, but one of them is more popularly known today as the Hymn of Jesus and was set to music a century ago by Gustav Holst. Here is quite a well-known section, in the translation by the Theosophist scholar, G. R. S. Mead. It takes the form of a simple hymn, beginning, 'Glory be to thee, Father', and continuing with the instruction:

And we, going about in a ring, answered him:

Amen.

Glory be to thee, Word:
Glory be to thee, Grace.

Amen.
Glory be to thee, Spirit:
Glory be to thee, Holy One:
Glory be to thy glory.
Amen.
We praise thee, O Father;
we give thanks to thee, O Light,
wherein darkness dwelleth not.
Amen.

I must repeat that we do not know that this had a Cathar use, but it is impossible to ignore the phrase, 'We give thanks to thee, O Light, wherein darkness dwelleth not', for it is so Cathar in sentiment.* It would give the basis of a liturgy centred on the real presence of Light in life. It would also bear out something I have tried to argue in my contribution to THE CATHAR VIEW entitled 'Cathar Joy', which is that Catharism is not gloomy — outside some of the cosmology of the 'Book of John' and another dualist text known as the 'Book of Two Principles'. I believe

*The connection with the Acts of John is taken up again below (pp. 48 and 73), in articles that repeat the Hymn of Jesus connection and add a new one, which has to do with the crucifixion story. For these words see chapter 94 of the text.

that Cathars had a real awareness of, an experience of, the thing that was not darkness, namely light. It takes only a little imagination to see this hymn as a ritual, and an ecstatic one.

Let's return to the Acts of John, whether or not they are a true Cathar source. Here is part of the introduction to them from one of the great repositories of Gnostic texts, the website of the Gnostic Society Library:

'The Acts of John is an early second-century Christian collection of Johannine narratives and traditions, long known in fragmentary form. The traditional author was said to be one Leucius Charinus, a companion and disciple of John. The Acts of John is considered one of the most significant of the apocryphal apostolic Acts. It preserves strains of early oral traditions about the "beloved disciple" and sole apostolic author of a canonical gospel text.

'The Acts of John describe (possibly apocryphal) journeys of John, tales filled with dramatic and miraculous events, anecdotes and well-framed apostolic speeches.'

(http://gnosis.org/library/hymnjesu.html)

It is tantalizing not to know how many of

these stories of journeys and miracles were known to the Cathars. Oral traditions have strengths and weaknesses: they keep an enormous amount alive – 'within the tradition' – but they can never be quantified, catalogued or relied upon. Nonetheless, we can be fairly certain that there will have been an oral tradition around John and known to the Cathars, whether or not it had written form, with texts such as these 'Acts'.

I'd therefore like to make a short summary of what we know about John, first from the Bible, secondly from early tradition, and thirdly from a developing tradition over the centuries through to the present. As far as the biblical tradition is concerned, we can – very fortunately – simply step around modern scholarly argument about whether St John the author of the gospel, St John the apostle and St John the writer of Revelation were the same person or not. That distinction will have had almost no meaning for the Cathars; all we need is to remember that fact.

The author of St John's gospel tells us no less than five times that John was 'the disciple Jesus loved'. He also holds a special place in the Bible because of the number of times he alone was present with Jesus, or in a very small group with Peter and maybe his brother James. These include the raising of Jairus's daughter, but also the Transfiguration (very significantly, in the context of what I have said about Mt Tabor). He and Peter enter Jerusalem together to prepare for the Last Supper, and at that first 'Love Feast' he leans on Jesus' breast. He remains alone with his Master at Calvary, and is with the two Marys at the Crucifixion. As Jesus is crucified there is the immensely touching ceremony in which Jesus commends his mother into John's care, and John into his mother's (*Woman, behold thy son...*, John 19 : 26–7). Jesus says some tantalizing things to Peter which seem to imply that John will linger on earth after the other disciples have died (*If I will that he tarry till I come, what is that to thee?*, John 21 : 23). He is the first to believe that Jesus is truly arisen, having been one of the first two disciples at the tomb, again with Peter. He is the first to recognize Jesus at the incident of the miraculous draft of fishes, after the resurrection. He takes a prominent part in the founding and guidance of the young Church in Acts of the Apostles.

So, let's next look at what the non-biblical tradition tells us, early on. First, he is known to have been present at the first Apostolic Council in AD 51. It seems highly likely that John went to Ephesus in Turkey once the disciples went their separate ways, preaching the gospel. Some authorities say he was later banished to the Isle of Patmos, which is convenient because the author of Revelation locates himself there. There is a strong tradition that, the youngest of the Twelve, he survived the rest of the apostles and lived to a great age.

John's traditional symbol slowly emerges as the eagle, with the explanation that the first verses of his gospel fly so high in their philosophical scope. Amalgamating the stories in the Acts of John with an early oral tradition occasionally written down, we surmise that John fulfilled his promise to Jesus and continued to look after Mary, the mother of Jesus, until her death in AD 54. In the Acts of John, he and Mary Magdalene then travel north into Asia Minor and settle in Ephesus. His date of death is sometimes given as AD 100, when he was 94.

Later traditions link John to the chalice

used at the Last Supper – probably because of a verse in St Matthew, 'My chalice indeed you shall drink' (20 : 23). This chalice symbolism, and its link with John, become widespread in art in the thirteenth century – significantly, at the time of the Cathars. The depth of meaning in the phrase from St Matthew can scarcely have been lost on the Cathar believers, and Jesus is quite clear in the gospels that when he uses words like 'cup' he means the receptacle of life-experience.

Lastly, as our harpist today, Ani Williams, observes in her chapter in THE CATHAR VIEW, the chalice symbol gets connected to the legend that St John was handled a cup of poisoned wine from which, at his blessing, the poison rose out in the shape of a serpent. This green snake becomes a regular device to denote John in art.

The tradition that St John never died is part of a purely esoteric tradition, but its first literary manifestation is probably the account of the life of the ecstatic nun Anne-Catharine Emmerich, who lived from 1774 to 1824. This is her vision:

'I also saw on another occasion that the body of St John did not remain on earth. I saw, between the West and the North, a place as radiant as a sun and I saw John there as an intermediary receiving something from on high to pass on to us. This place, although it seemed to me very high and completely inaccessible, was nonetheless part of the world.'

(The whole of Anne-Catherine Emmerich's vision is available in English online at *http:// tandfspi.org/ACE_misc/ACE_misc_capsule_out*.html)

White Eagle describes the relation of Jesus and John as being parallel to the relation of the human soul and the human spirit. He also moots the idea that John is the teacher of the New Age. And he confirms the esoteric tradition that John, like Jesus, did not die but was in some way lifted into heaven without going through the process of death.

I have suggested in my article, 'Cathar Joy', that members of the Polaire brotherhood of the 1930s, who were Grace Cooke's French companions at Lordat, may have recognized in Catharism teaching about how to come through the gates of death without any sense of a change of state. Otto Rahn wrote that to be a true Cathar without having lived earthly life in vain, you needed 'to divinize life in such a way that at the moment of death, the body abandons this world without regrets'; while the more general Polaire charge was so to live that you helped others overcome 'the mad fear of death that haunts the mind of man'. 'Pourquoi donc trembler, au seuil des Portes de la Lumière?' – 'why should any of us tremble, on the threshold of the Gates of Light?'.

And so we return to the trip to Ariège in 1931, and my grandmother's vision. Can the account of St John commencing the Cathar tradition be dismissed as an absurdity? There is no more *scholarly* justification for it at the end of my paper than there was at the beginning. There are, maybe, just a few more reasons why we might take it seriously. I have only briefly, for instance, mentioned Mary Magdalene. An ancient French oral tradition around St-Lazare of Bethany and Les Saintes-Maries in Provence is that the two Marys, Mary Magdalene's brother Lazarus and another of the seventy apostles named Maximinus landed in Provence after a crossing from the Holy Land in a frail boat without a mast. Two things would link John with this: either the tradition, carried forward by St Jerome, that Mary of Magdala and St John were betrothed, or another tradition, which is that he and Lazarus were the same person. Or, of course, a third tradition, but I believe this is more modern, that Mary and John were the same person. Certain Cathar records, of course, do describe a Cathar belief that Jesus was married to this Mary; we do not know how widespread this belief was in the Languedoc.

As to the actual vision, one thing that for me gives it a certain stature is this. I am quite certain that when Grace Cooke took up the Polaires' request to accompany them to the Pyrenees, she knew so little about these devoted brethren from the middle ages that she would certainly have known nothing about how great a stress Cathars placed on the story and teaching of St John. She could have learnt it from the Polaires, but very recently, and to place the responsibility on them is only to transfer the question elsewhere. Zam Bhotiva would have known of the Cathars as Johannine in character from his fellow Polaire Maurice Magre, who had written the book that has since become popular in English as THE RETURN OF THE MAGI, and who wrote of the 'Johannnine Church of the

Cathars' in the Polaire *Bulletin*.* She was told in England by Ivan Cooke's guide that she would be the only one to find the treasure, and I think the treasure was the contact she made. That was certainly what she believed later, when the vision was assimilated.

I've argued in my 'Joy' article that although those in the Polaire group who were at the more ignorant end of commitment may really have expected them all to find buried treasure, I think it is highly unlikely that Zam Bhotiva and the 'Mage' of the Polaires (Mario Fille, who remained in Paris) had any such illusion. They understood too well the teaching they followed, which came to them through the Oracle of Astral Force.* Bhotiva, I am convinced, knew only that my grandmother had to be got to Lordat for the spiritual connection she would make there. And as I have stated earlier in the article, I believe that making such a connection was the real beginning of the White Eagle Lodge work.

*This article can be read in English translation in THE CATHAR VIEW, pp. 187–90.   † For further explanation, see ASIA MYSTERIOSA, mentioned above, p. 16.

Proud to be Heretical

The White Eagle Cathar: 1 (Stella Polaris, *August* 2013)

MANY READERS of this magazine will be aware that I have recently been studying the thirteenth-century emergence of 'heresy' that is known as Catharism. White Eagle's followers may have been called heretics themselves often enough to have no problem with that word – but popular use of it is of course a manifestation of that well-known saying, 'history is written by the victors'. Indeed, it's doubtful if any set of Christian beliefs can be regarded as truly orthodox: they have simply been defined as such by those who held the greatest sway in the various councils and synods set up to normalize Christian doctrine. It may just be that what was squashed out of the Church then, so violently, was a sweetness and a closeness of persons, one to another, that a heavily-defended organization could not stand. The Cathars' subtle authenticity (another way of expressing the same phenomenon) is what this new series of articles will be about.

My own interest in these people goes back to conversations I first overheard in my childhood, and then engaged in, with Minesta (Grace Cooke). She would speak of the visit she made to the south of France – the Pyrenees, she would sometimes loosely say – in 1931, and at the mention of the geographical focus of her trip, the château at Lordat, in the department of Ariège, her voice would become soft and her eyes would fill with the joyous distance. That memory was enough to get me there with my mother and brother around 1980, and since then I must have been back to the area eight or nine times, leading groups on a number of those occasions. I have written about my grandparents' trip there in the article I wrote for the cathar view entitled 'A visit to Ariège in 1931'.

'Why should the Cathars be of interest in the White Eagle work?' is a slightly different question from 'Why do the Cathars have so much hold over people's imagination today?' and it's that first one I'm wanting to answer. This series of articles will take the connections one at a time, but let's begin with a summary. First, the visit that Minesta and Brother Faithful* made in July 1931 has every reason to be regarded as the starting point of our work. Some day, I'd love to see an astrological chart for the Lodge based on that time. Second, the vision Minesta had at Lordat, largely reprinted in THE LIVING WORD OF ST JOHN but in full in THE CATHAR VIEW, gives us a whole new insight into the origins of Catharism. Third, White Eagle has a number of times indicated that those who work in the Lodge may have had incarnations in the Cathar brotherhood and come together again in the Lodge as a group reincarnation. Fourth, that word 'brotherhood' is one with extraordinary resonance and significance in our work; fifth, understanding the Cathars gives us a window on our forbears the Polaire brethren, and sixth, the habits and lifestyle of the Cathars, the things

*These are the names by which Grace and Ivan Cooke were generally known within the White Eagle Lodge. The moment might be said to be the start of the work because the realization of St John as one whose authority lay behind White Eagle's was what enabled Grace Cooke to commit to the whole undertaking with which she seems to have been entrusted by spirit.

they believed in, have the deepest relevance for Lodge members today.

I've now used the word 'Catharism' twice and shall continue doing so, and yet it is a profoundly misleading one. In the first place, the Cathars never used any such word to identify themselves; it was the way their enemies described them. The word comes from the Greek *katharoi*, meaning 'pure ones' but it also has a *double entendre* which was meant to be heard. Cathars, by contrast, only recognized each other as *bonshommes*, 'good men' – and good women too, for they did not discriminate between the sexes in the way the church they rejected did. They were also *les bons chrétiens*, 'the good Christians', recognizing in their traditions a direct but unorthodox lineage back to Apostolic times.

The second point is that they were no '-ism' either. Modern scholarship has turned to recognizing them as something that developed more or less spontaneously as a revolt against the corrupt church they were forced to accept, and to which the Church then attached a name indiscriminately. That viewpoint, which allows much less influence to their historical precursors, re-

mains controversial, but what comes out of it is a sense of local communities rebelling against excesses and re-establishing a pure way of worship, rejecting the church both doctrinally and as a system of local government in the process.*
Cathars were free, and sought to explore their own direct relationship with God through the person of the Holy Spirit above all. Later, as a result of persecution, there was more organization and structure — but that was reactive, not the natural choice of the Cathar.

Why is this last point of interest to us? Well, I personally find it helpful because White Eagle speaks of 'the Cathar brotherhood', yet that term 'brotherhood' has sat uneasily with what scholarship has traditionally told us. The new historians' perspective sees those who rejected the Church's authority as self-contained groups within individual communities, people who

*Predominant in the revisionist view is R. I. Moore, whose book THE WAR ON HERESY (London, Profile Books, 2012) details the way in which the Church suddenly turned itself on the defensive and then onto the attack, against those whose ideas did not conform. Moore's thesis has been strongly resisted in other quarters, but the 'localism' of Cathar communities is not in particular question.

knew one another well and trusted one another enough to keep secrets and not betray identities. That's a model much more likely to produce something to which the name 'brotherhood' might here and there be fairly attached – wherever the ideal and the wisdom was strong enough to support the concept. Every community was different, and doubtless true brotherhood existed in the most enlightened ones, or when an enlightened individual offered leadership, and rather less in others. Such a genesis certainly seems to have applied when Catharism was revived by the Authié brothers in Ax-les-Thermes in the last decade of the thirteenth century, although that revival had very clear doctrines that we know about. Doctrinal emphasis differed between one village, or town, and another, and it even differed between the brothers Authié.

It's not unreasonable (whatever our theories from history) to see the story of the Cathars as falling into three phases. In the first, there was spontaneous association of individuals within communities, sharing both positive beliefs and the need to withdraw, whether publicly or dis-

PROUD TO BE HERETICAL

creetly, from the Church. The second is the one
in which, faced with persecution (first a crusade and then an inquisition), these groups became significantly more organized and bishops
were appointed, following a visit from a Bogomil elder from Bulgaria – the slightly earlier
Bogomils sharing similar beliefs. This period
symbolically ends with the fall of Montségur
and the supposed extirpation of the heresy in
the decade following. Yet then there is the third
period, the revival just mentioned, which began
around 1295 and continued just fifteen years –
to 1310 in France, though a decade longer in
Spain. White Eagle readers may have a special
interest in this last phenomenon, since it began
and was based in precisely the region that Minesta was called to, the Ariège.

Communities traditionally bond under external threat, but modern community-building
theories emphasize that the measure of real
community is its inclusivity.* Only very de-

*The starting point for any study of modern community-
building theory is M. Scott Peck's THE DIFFERENT DRUM (London, Arrow Books, 1987). The theme continues in articles
4 and 5 in the series (below, pp. 59–71).

tailed scholarship could track the tiny communities one by one, but two things stand out. One
is the Cathars' strict espousal of non-violence, a
principle that they interpreted as never doing
anything to hurt another human being. Such
a doctrine speaks well of Cathar communities
looking after their more marginal members:
those who in traditional society, through learning or physical disability, through personality
difficulties, through racial minority, and so on,
tend to become outcasts. It is one of the things
that makes the Cathars so rare and so precious.

This is backed up by point number two,
which is the reputation the Cathars had for in-
tegration with local Jewish and Islamic groups.
There is at least some reason to believe that they
learnt from Jewish Cabalism and the Sufi ele-
vation of spiritual love, so neither is this sur-
prising.* Both it and Cathar non-violence are,
however, absolutely outstanding: where else in
Europe for centuries before and after could we
find the same?

Whence came the strength to follow prin-

*The possible link with Sufism is taken up again in article
9 in this series, on p. 91.

ciples that carried such risk of personal injury at the hands of a persecutor? Whence came the intensity of love that brought such discipline to a society whose only hierarchies were based on initiation? That is what my next article will explore.

O Shadowless Light

The White Eagle Cathar: 2 (October 2013)

Glory be to thee, Word:
Glory be to thee, Grace.
Amen.
Glory be to thee, Spirit:
Glory be to thee, Holy One:
Glory be to thy glory.
Amen.
We praise thee, O Father;
we give thanks to thee, O Light,
wherein darkness dwelleth not.
Amen.

IN A TEACHING that appears in this issue,* White Eagle refers intriguingly to 'the hymn and dance of Jesus'. He is almost certainly referring to a text commonly known as 'The Hymn

*The relevant passage is offered in the Appendix, below, p. 108. For the source of the opening quotation, see p. 28

of Jesus', which was and is best known for comprising most of the libretto for Gustav Holst's choral work of that name, his next composition after The Planets. In fact, the 'Hymn of Jesus' is a section from an early Gnostic text known as 'The Acts of John'. Its date is not known precisely, but it was being quoted by the end of the second century, so it is very early. The section in which it appears is headed 'The Hymn of the Lord Which he sang in Secret to the Holy Apostles, his Disciples'.

Are we hearing words here that were loved (albeit in Latin) by the Cathars as well as (apparently) by White Eagle, maybe somehow bearing out his oft-spoken longing to see us all 'dancing a divine dance'? We actually can't make that a statement, because there is no evidence of 'The Acts of John' survived as a Cathar text. On the other hand, one thing that we do know is that Cathars revered the writings of St John over all the other Gospels, to the extent that every practising Cathar carried a copy of John's Gospel with him or her, at all times. They had other 'heretical' works linked to John, and it would be very attractive to believe that they had this too.

The words are an ecstatic celebration of divine life, by Jesus, immediately prior to his being given over to the High Priests. Or so they claim, thus demonstrating a gnostic revelation, the special understanding that the Gnostics sought. The key phrase for us is 'O light In whom darkness dwells not', rendered in Gustav Holst's text as 'O shadowless light!'.

Scholarship tends to imply that the Cathars were deeply imbued with a worldview which saw the world as irredeemably dark, and something that could only be overcome by the complete abandonment of worldly attachment. I have long felt this does no justice at all to what Cathars may well have felt, but were never asked by the Inquisition to describe, namely an abundant sense of the reality and power of the light that contrasted darkness, and of the soul's ability to dwell in that consciousness. Nearly all our records come from the Inquisitors, yet nothing else but this explains the radiance that is recorded from those who went to the flames for their belief: nothing besides a revelation of what lay ahead of them: a birth into absolute light.

Once this belief is taken on, that some Cathars (see my first article, implying that there were many separate groups or even 'brotherhoods' of Cathars, maybe with different levels of understanding) had a real awareness and experience of light, and not just of earthly darkness, the connection with White Eagle's teaching today falls completely into place. White Eagle longs, I believe, for us all to open our eyes to the beauties of the heaven world and to realize that they are manifest here and now, not far away. We need to learn to live in the light precisely so that like the Cathars we can, when death comes, walk radiantly into it, and so that our very living on the earth is an act of bringing down into matter the light of spirit. We are the channels by which the earth is transformed.

The other relevance of the little passage quoted is that it reminds us of the person of St John himself. Not a lot is known of John after the resurrection and ascension of Jesus, except that he was one of the most active of the disciples – as befits one who had been so close to Jesus as to be 'beloved'. There is reasonable evidence to believe he based himself with Mary the mother of Jesus, lived in Ephesus, in Turkey, and continued to live to a very considerable age. There is even a tradition, which White Eagle honours, that John did not die in the normal way (or in a violent way, like so many of the disciples) but underwent some form of transition similar to Jesus's ascension. What a story to inspire the Cathars, with their beliefs, if they were aware of it!

I cannot here quote the vision that Minesta had at Lordat in 1931, mentioned last time, but it is in the introduction to THE LIVING WORD OF ST JOHN (White Eagle Publishing Trust) or in a slightly fuller version in Polair Publishing's THE CATHAR VIEW (2012). In her vision Minesta was told by a Cathar brother that John came from where he was to the South of France and made contact there with some special influence. Later, members of the brotherhood he founded in the near East came to the same spot, and founded there the church of the inner teachings, the Cathar beliefs. It is a most powerful vision to hold.

Christmas to the Cathar

The White Eagle Cathar: 3 (December 2013)

IT IS PRESENTLY the Christmas season, and so it might be a fair question ask what Christmas meant to the Cathars. Alongside the question, it's good to remember that although Christmas has been celebrated in all sorts of different forms over the years, many of the most loved Christmas carols are mediaeval. Some of them have a strongly mystical outlook, too. It would be lovely to find the Cathars of the thirteenth century right in the middle of such a tradition – yet unfortunately, as far as I know, there is no reason to connect them with it at all. There is however an alternative musical tradition that they may be fairly linked to, which is that of the mediaeval troubadours – one that would give them a psychic space in which they might have celebrated the feminine traditions within Christian belief, and in particular the idealized adoration of women as an embodiment of the Divine Mother. That link has never been proven, but is immensely attractive, for some of the musical origins of the troubadours are Spanish – and that means Moorish Spain, and potentially Sufism, where love is similarly elevated.*

As far as I can understand, Cathars' understanding of Christmas would have been a little double-faceted. They are understood to have believed that the Son of God could not undergo earthly suffering, in the form of crucifixion especially. They tended to a belief that there was a spiritual being semi-separate from the human one, within the framework of 'Jesus Christ'. The earthly being could suffer, but it could not express the absolute glory of the Christ life. The divine being represented a total manifestation of God visible to human beings, but one that was untarnishable. The resurrection was the triumph of this being, and its ascension a crucial element of Cathar faith.

Take out some of the extremes of light and dark, and Cathar belief seems so close to what

*This topic is taken up again in the ninth article, on p. 91, below.

White Eagle teaches! The divine being of Christ is surely our 'Cosmic Christ' – the one whom Jesus made visible, through embodiment – without trapping that being into fleshly thrall. Christmas, to White Eagle (as I understand him), celebrates the birth at one and the same moment of an earthly babe and a divine being. Each is without power unless the other is present within it, and the angels come together in adoration of both. White Eagle reminds us that the Christ Mass is an event celebrated as much in heaven as on earth, and his Inner Teaching in this issue* is one of his most profound statements on that subject.

There is something else to learn from the Cathars at this time, too. Immersion in Cathar doctrines led sooner or later to a desire to receive what was known as the *consolamentum*. We might call it an initiation. At its deepest, the *consolamentum* celebrated the total removal of the candidate or appellant from earthly connection. He or she was so completely reinvented through that initiation and through the training that preceded it

*See Appendix, p. 108

that the Inquisition referred cynically to the re-born Cathar as *parfait* or *perfectus* — implying that they believed themselves perfect.*

If they did, it was a different sort of perfection from the one their detractors probably understood by it. In language, a perfect tense represents an action completed. The initiated Cathar had completed transformation to the extent that he or she took on all that went with being like the 'higher' Christ. To be a *parfait* was to have completed earthly experience, apart from living out the present incarnation, and to express the divine completely; to know nothing but the expression of the higher world upon earth. It was to love others unconditionally and without exception. Catharism, you might say, was like our Lodge an attempt '*to bring into being on the earth plane a standard of life which is in harmony with the infinite love*'.

What Christmas celebrates, most deeply, is the revelation that every human being can be born again. No, not in the evangelical sense of today, which I suppose links very much with the earthly Jesus, but born again into an absolutely

*See below, article 10, for more on the *consolamentum*.

changed consciousness. When White Eagle says, 'You are spirit first and body last', he is being a most excellent Cathar. But St Matthew also, two thousand years ago, quotes Jesus as saying, *Let your light so shine before men, that they may see your good works, and glorify your Father which is in heaven* (Matthew 5 : 16). And in a chapter of St John that must have been of enormous significance to Cathar minds, Jesus says, *He that believeth on me, the works that I do shall he do also; and greater works than these shall he do; because I go unto my Father* (14 : 12).

In short, to be born again a 'good Christian' by virtue of the *consolamentum* was to take on the role of Christ himself. The *parfait* attained the right to say the Lord's Prayer, which only one who had such a role could say (something our view of the Middle Ages often ignores). Yet when he or she said the phrase *On earth as it is in heaven* the *parfait* took that to mean that there was no distinction between the two. Once you had taken on the consciousness of higher being there was nothing else.

The Christmas story is a most wonderful one, and it retells (according to White Eagle) a mystery of being that has been true since the beginning of human time. Not just the birth of a child in a stable two thousand years ago; the birth of a complete renewal of consciousness within the human being, which has happened since time immemorial. As White Eagle tells us, 'You are spirit in an earthly body, and spirit is free, deathless and divine as its origin'.

Transfiguration

The White Eagle Cathar: 4 (February 2014)

AT THE TIME of writing, rosy dawn has been uplifting up the December sky, its pale and special light continuing on into the morning. For me, it brings memories of the special mountain that sits between Montségur and Lordat, which is called the Pic de St-Barthélémy, and which I feel I have seen more than once in similar light. Its alternative name is the Montagne de Tabe, and that has has been linked to Mount Tabor in the Holy Land, the mountain of the Transfiguration.

Somehow this light, both today and then, is transfiguring. It lifts us beyond our troubles and takes us into a place of the upper elements, including the pink fire that the clouds are painted with. Cathars must have crossed the Tabe massif in the morning light, often, and must have looked many times at the sky and wondered what the future held – only to remember that they were, just as White Eagle tells us we are, 'spirit first and body last'. Maybe they felt reassurance that spirit was a realm of infinite love. So what was to come did not really matter: only that that knowledge, of being spirit, and the goodness of it, was kept alive.

The image is pertinent as our own London Lodge 'sets out on its travels'.* How many fears are calmed and pacified by that true knowledge of a loving spirit? How real for us is calling on that process now! I believe that words elsewhere in this issue of *Stella Polaris*† show how far members of the London Lodge recognize what is true, which is that their community is a bonding one with another around shared belief, and is not tied to the building we are leaving.

It's a yielding we have no choice but to ac-

*When this was written, it was assumed that the sale of the London Lodge in Kensington, W8, would happen within a month or so, and we were about to move to temporary premises. The sale did not take place till the following August, but even then a new permanent home had not been found, and the Lodge activities moved temporarily to the Quaker Meeting House in St Martin's Lane, in London's West End.   †To bear out the point, these are reproduced in Appendix I (pp. 109–112).

cept, just as the early brethren of the Lodge did when they left their home of Burstow Manor in 1935, and the bombed site of Pembroke Hall, the first White Eagle Lodge building, in 1940. Yet Cathars owned no buildings. They did not believe that manmade things could be consecrated. At most, a room in a farmhouse or a hilltop château could be quickly transformed into a place of light by the addition of candles and any other burning flame that could be found. Those who lead White Eagle meetings in rented premises are re-enacting something from the thirteenth century when they put the room together for whatever ritual they will hold.

There is community and there is ritual, and memories go deep in both. The Cathars believed that their rituals were more strictly in accord with those of Apostolic times than were those of the Church, and we too pride ourselves that our own rituals reflect brotherhoods of old – from our method of healing, to our services, to the ritual of our own Brotherhood meeting. The *consolamentum*, best known of the Cathar rituals, was effectively a fire initiation, in which those burning lights, everywhere, had great significance. Fire relates to courage, and to love – both of them called into play to their extreme when a Cathar life ended in a burning at the stake, which thankfully ours do not, in any literal sense.

For many White Eagle people, their sense of awe around a particular place links as much to the outdoors as to interior spaces – or ones which blend the two. Stonehenge brings us memories of great ceremonies, and so does a much smaller monument, the one known as the West Kennet Long Barrow. My brother Jeremy once wrote in this magazine of his experience at the latter, feeling that in that place there was no real separation between earth and spirit. White Eagle expressed a similar hope when he called the Temple at New Lands a meeting point between heaven and earth. And Minesta, visiting the château at Lordat in 1931, had an encounter with a Brother whose very quality of presence linked her both to the Cathars and to St John, whom the Brother told her was the real founder of the Cathar brotherhood. I believe myself that a place, with memories, can indeed be such a window.

St John guides our White Eagle work as well as that of the Cathars, and at unseen and sometimes visible levels. John was given a sacred task to look after his Mother Mary by Jesus, and John and Mary offer a very simple male–female paradigm for the dual ritual which survives in our Sunday services. Another feature of the early church was the *agape*, or love feast, which is older than the Eucharist. It was a communal meal, based on the Last Supper, and the sharing of bread certainly brought spirit into the gathering. But spirit was there precisely because it was shared: people came together in their joint experience of the presence of Jesus. Spirit was present in their love one for another, just as Jesus had commanded. Transubstantiation* came as a later doctrine.

This article is intended to tie closely, I confess, with the experience of community set out collectively by London Lodge members in the feature I mentioned earlier.† Cathars bonded in

---

*'The change whereby, according to the teaching of the Catholic Church, the bread and the wine used in the sacrament of the Eucharist become, not merely as by a sign or a figure, but also in actual reality the body and blood of Christ. †See note on p. 60

the same way: all of us, the early Church, the Cathars and the Lodge community, come together when they share bread – today, it's more often a potluck meal than bread and wine (here my mind goes happily to activities at the American and Australasian centres as much as to London). Yet our purpose, 'to bring into being on the earth plane a standard of life which is in harmony with the infinite love', is just as lofty.

The Cathars sometimes shocked the Inquisitors by their (apparently) very free view of human connectedness, and their judges accused them of all sorts of perversions. I believe that to be enlightened by initiation, and henceforth to share totally, was what distinguished the Cathars. I wonder whether we in the Lodge are, in fact, in a unique position to understand what they really believed, and wonder if it lay somewhere in a recognition that since the *parfait* contained nothing but God in him or her, any assembly blessed with the presence of *parfaits* could elevate a simple community of human beings to a true love-feast, a spiritual celebration and communion by ones who valued their connectedness over and above their individual needs?

My thoughts return to earth, and to the now grey sky. What, I wonder, will an enlightened traveller a hundred years hence pick up, in the atmosphere, when he or she stands at the site that the London Lodge occupied from 1941 to 2014?

A Very Aquarian Brotherhood

The White Eagle Cathar: 5 (April 2014)

AT THE BEGINNING of this series, last August, I stated that 'the Cathars' subtle authenticity' was what these articles would be about. I hope I have held to that; the present article explores, among other things, what 'authenticity' might actually mean in this context.

One of the ways in which the Cathars stand out as an example, and maybe appeal today, is the almost total absence of hierarchy within their religious structure, so far as we know. We read of *credentes*, believers, and *perfecti*, initiated ones, but these were not ranks so much as identifiers used by the Inquisitors. The former were the simple adherents who had taken no vows but were linked to the cause and in some cases died for it, and the latter were those who had passed through what is sometimes (I believe misleadingly) compared to an ordination and which I have characterized instead as a profound initiation. It was known as the *consolamentum*.

Although those who had received the rite of *consolamentum* were instructors in a tradition, mentors to those entering training, ministers to the sick and devoted consolers of the dying, they formed no part of a structured system because there was none. The *parfaits* (as *perfecti* were called in French) were revered, and they led confessions, but in no sense did they form a priesthood. Nor did they look up to any rank above them. At a certain point in Cathar history, it is true, five bishops were appointed; yet this act is generally regarded today as a response to persecution, when there arose a need to have an area organizer, someone who could warn and direct, not someone who held sway over lesser orders.*

This much I intimated in my first article, but it leaves us with a most notable fact. First we must ask, if the Cathars had no organizational hierarchy, did they function by a sort of guru

*Cathar practice, as described here, very beautifully anticipates the church of the new age described by White Eagle in THE LIGHT BRINGER (White Eagle Publishing Trust, second edition, 2015; see especially pp. 53, 63–4)

principle, in which noted teachers acted as leaders by example and inspirers of others? To some extent the *parfaits* do seem to have held an exemplary role, but if this represented conventional leadership, the first thing we should expect is for key names to have been recorded. Provocatively, I would ask, 'Name me an important Cathar'. With mythology behind you, you might mention Esclarmonde de Foix; with knowledge of the siege of Montségur you might recognize the names of Bertrand Marty and Pierre-Roger de Mirepoix; if you had read recent studies from Inquisition records you would come up with quite a few names from the 1295–1310 revival, and most likely its inspirers, the brothers Authié or Authier. That would likely be all.

To an extent, at least, one of the distinctions of that late revival is that it seems to have been consciously initiated by the Authié family: but though they certainly led by example the distinction itself emphasizes how without leaders the early period of Catharism was. The notable fact is that we are witnessing here, seven hundred years before the concept became recognized as an option, a truly leaderless community – leaderless at the least in any hierarchical sense.*

Belief itself, maybe, offered a form of leadership, in individual and even isolated communities linked only by scorn for the corrupt church and (we in the Lodge might add) some unexplained local ownership of a Christianity that adherents knew in their hearts was more 'authentic' in its rites and in its doctrines than an organized Church with twelve or thirteen hundred years of theology to support it. They apparently knew that the Church Fathers had developed the doctrine of transubstantiation, but that the Apostles knew only a Love Feast, *agape* in Greek, which mimicked the Last Supper quite strictly. Cathars seem to have followed the simple shared meal, the *agape*. As the disciples looked to a Master who had been with them 'a

*The revival at the end of the thirteenth century is the subject of the intriguing study by René Weis, THE YELLOW CROSS : THE STORY OF THE LAST CATHARS 1290–1329 (London, Viking, 2000). The characters met in this study are other names we might recall, though hardly leaders; the book reminds us that however much we look at people in ideal terms, there is an earthly history in which they seem very different.

little while' and then was known in arisen form, the Cathars maybe looked to discarnate examples and long-preserved rites and memories to guide them, recognizing those who had passed on before and absolutely revering the teaching they seemed to have had from nature and from – dare we even suggest it? – a local tradition of love one for another that held something any number of Papal reforms could not emulate.

And authenticating that statement, for us White Eagle Cathars today, is the big question. Our beloved founder, Grace Cooke, in 1931 had a vision at the château of Lordat. The village is right in the area of the Authié revival and may have been a site for earlier Catharism too. Minesta had a visionary encounter there that was very specific, and almost unique, in that it leads to the conclusion that Catharism was special because the beloved disciple, John, had travelled to the South of France in his long lifetime, returned to Ephesus and there founded a brotherhood that upheld the earliest Christian traditions in simple community. This brotherhood then sent its branches West again, back to the place that John had so evidently loved.

In White Eagle terms, it is this account that leads us to talk about 'the Cathar brotherhood', however much that term might be frowned on by scholars. Our own attachment to St John as the founder of Catharism is not generally accepted, and yet our unique understanding here does at least one useful thing: it gives a line of descent for those simple, authentic beliefs from the time of the Apostles to the time of the Cathars. And it would explain why the Cathars, for their part, revered St John like no other.

Raised Up

The White Eagle Cathar: 6 (June 2014)

ONE OF the verses from St John's gospel that White Eagle quotes most frequently is chapter 12, verse 32: 'I, if I be lifted up, will raise all men unto me'. It has always puzzled me slightly how White Eagle feels able to use it to imply that if we, like Jesus, rise into our higher consciousness, it is then that we will raise all beings with us: in fact, the very next verse of the gospel reads, 'This he said, signifying what death he should die' – presumably, by being lifted up on the cross. Those may not be St John's own words (they sound 'editorial'), but they do seem to contradict White Eagle's interpretation, hence my worry.

There is a text that I connected at least indirectly with the Cathars in my second article, and which possibly explains why White Eagle should feel able to ignore this straightforward explanation. I mentioned that the apocryphal

Acts of John was already being quoted in the second century AD, so it was written not a lot later than the canonical gospels. It includes the words known as the 'Hymn of Jesus', which begins, 'Glory to Thee, Word!', a poetic sequence that I quoted before.

After the Hymn of Jesus section, the Acts of John proceeds to relate a vision that John had of Jesus at the moment of the 'sixth hour' of the Crucifixion, when 'darkness fell over all the land' (Matthew 27 : 45). He at once saw 'my Lord standing in the midst of the cave and enlightening it'. Jesus explains that to the multitude he is visibly being crucified, but if John will attend to what he says, he will be able to come up the mountain with Jesus and hear special teaching.

Jesus then shows John a cross of light set up above the multitude who surround the wooden cross. John sees Jesus above the cross, speaking in 'a voice not such as was familiar to us, but one sweet and kind and truly of God, saying unto me, "John ... this cross of light is sometimes called the word by me for your sakes, sometimes mind, sometimes Jesus, sometimes Christ, sometimes door, sometimes a way, sometimes bread, sometimes seed, sometimes resurrection, sometimes Son, sometimes Father, sometimes Spirit, sometimes life, sometimes truth, sometimes faith, sometimes grace ... it is ... the firm uplifting of things fixed out of things unstable, and the harmony of wisdom"'.*

In short, and if my understanding is correct, Jesus is demonstrating a cross of light above the wooden cross which shows that it is the way out of the limited earthly world into the consciousness of the divine life. The vision amply illustrates the tradition in which White Eagle is speaking when he gives the interpretation he does of 'I, if I be lifted up'.

Some Cathars were puzzled and in many ways repulsed by the idea of the crucifixion (I remember that my mother, who had Cathar memories, was, too), because they could not believe that the divine Jesus could suffer earthly humiliation and mortality. They thus developed a dualistic idea of an earthly being raised to the highest pinnacle of humanness, and a spiritual being whose light reached down and touched the one in the dark-

*Acts of John, chapter 98, quoted from the online version at http://gnosis.org/library/actjohn.htm

– 74 –

ness below. The story I have quoted, with its cross of light above the cross of wood, is one of the reasons that it is attractive to regard the Acts of John as known to the Cathars, although there is no record extant to confirm this. Most significantly, we understand through the link made here that White Eagle's sense of a universal Christ holding some degree of separateness from the earthly Jesus is one remarkably like a Cathar belief, and one evidently held by the early Johannine tradition very, very soon after the time of Jesus.

It is generally accepted that St John accepted the charge given him by Jesus to take care of his mother, Mary (John 19 : 27) and, when the disciples dispersed, went with her to Ephesus in Asia Minor. The vision that Minesta had at Lordat in the Pyrenean foothills takes up from this point. The shining Brother whom she perceived to be from Cathar times told her that St John had come to the Languedoc and returned to Asia Minor to form a brotherhood. This brotherhood then in part migrated back to the south of France, and represented the origin of the Cathars. Almost no other authority, scholarly or intuitive/psychic, repeats this story, and yet the strong influence of Johannine thought upon the Cathars is undeniable.

In the distinction between the physical cross and the cross of light, the physical-world Jesus and the spiritual-world Christ, I suggest we have a clear pointer as to how to deal with Cathar dualism. Not by a heavy concentration on the evil world, as I believe comes across from some scholarship, but as a way to raise the consciousness to the extent we focus on the light. The Cathar *parfait* was one who, having received the *consolamentum*, never again needed to rely on earth for support, but was born as Christ was, spiritual only. '*He shall give you another Comforter*' (John 14 : 16) must have meant everything to the Cathar. We find the notion of the Comforter again in White Eagle, as in the first teaching in this issue.*

Maurice Magre, one of those whom Minesta may have met in Paris among the Polaires, wrote in the Polaire *Bulletin* of the Cathars as the Johannine church† and the Roman Catholic as

---

*This is the White Eagle teaching headed 'The White Dove', in the June 2014 issue of *Stella Polaris*. See the excerpt in Appendix I, p. 112, below.
†See above, p. 9; Magre's article is on p. 187.

that of Peter. I am of the belief that that connection was newly made, in that very group
of devoted Brothers, and I suspect that having
come to this realization the rest of the Polaires,
in introducing Minesta to Cathar country, delib-
erately brought her under the ray of John. That
moment, I've said, is the starting point of our
work.

On the Run

The White Eagle Cathar: 7 (October 2014)

I'M WRITING this in Bulgaria, which is the home of the 'brotherhood' formed by Peter Deunov at the beginning of the twentieth century. 'The Teacher', as he is known, presented the world with the ritual movement or dance known as paneurhythmy, and it still continues despite years of persecution under both communist and fascist governments. To understand the level of devotion and fidelity which led the disciples of the Teacher to meet in remote mountain camps, escaping the gaze of the authorities, is also to gain a little window on how it must have been for the later Cathars to meet when they could, maybe for a *consolamentum* ceremony in a remote farmhouse. Always to meet under threat of discovery must be extraordinarily difficult for spiritual work. Imagine a healing service in the Lodge where some Big Brother

might at any time invade, arrest, close down …
but no, don't, for the perspective is unbearable.
We are fortunate, incredibly fortunate, to op-
erate (mainly) in parts of the world that offer
both tolerance and protection to our values.

Persecution is not however without its rec-
ompense. It offers a distinctly greater likelihood
of deep loyalty, in particular. Although there
were a few Cathars who became turncoats under
duress, this was rare, and one of the remarkable
aspects of Catharism was its solidarity within
groups which, being leaderless, were not held
together by any hierarchy or set of orders. Loyalty came from a recognition of what connected
me, a brother, with you, another brother. In the
case of a *parfait* it also came from the undertaking, as the *consolamentum* was administered, never
to forsake the faith nor to reveal the name of another brother. Yet the injunction was also never
to lie – a knife-edge the Cathar had to tread.

When persecution ends, we celebrate. We
start to establish ourselves in ways that more
or less guarantee onward protection. We build
foundations for the future – maybe quite literally. Numbers grow, our profile is better known,

but as a phrase in White Eagle's prayer for the Lodge reminds us, numbers are not everything. It's 'never to mistake numbers, praise or publicity for success'.

I think I could honestly say that wonderful though some of the large gatherings I've been to in the Lodge have been, some of the clearest contact with spirit that I have had has occurred in small groups. Spirit maybe manifests better, like a rich experience in meditation, when you least expect it.

There's a parallel with the time of Jesus here. Here is a verse from St John's Gospel I was reminded of recently, and which I found very touching. It is a moment recorded from after the crucifixion and resurrection.

'*Then the same day at evening, being the first day of the week, when the doors were shut where the disciples were assembled for fear of the Jews, came Jesus and stood in the midst, and saith unto them, Peace be unto you.*' (20 : 19)

I hadn't realized that no less than three times in this gospel chapter, when Jesus made such an appearance, he uttered the same words, '*Peace be unto you*'. A phrase of deep reassurance. It somehow put me back into memories of White Eagle speaking, rising from the chair no longer as Minesta, making a sign of the cross within the circle, and saying, from a space I scarcely valued in my youth for it came so frequently, 'Beloved brethren, we come amongst you from the world of light...'.

We don't know that such a presence of spirit as this was known to the Cathars as such – though they knew it well enough through St John – but what we do know is that at every opportunity they had to meet they looked back way beyond the Church of Rome to apostolic times and to the time of Jesus himself. They looked in simplicity at gatherings then which were maybe no larger than their own covert meetings. But we can be more specific. The Cathar carried a copy of St John's gospel, in Latin or in the vernacular, with him or her at all times. It was well-worn, I'm sure. Every word of St John's gospel left its imprint on Cathar belief, as I've tried to suggest here. Peter Deunov urged his Bulgarian disciples to read St John above all. With a teacher 'on the ray of John', we could surely at least bookmark St John's gospel on our iPads today! Or carry THE

LIVING WORD OF ST JOHN, or THE LIGHT BRINGER.*

The Cathars wandered, spreading their truth. Peter Deunov travelled Bulgaria for the first years of his ministry and never owned his own home or meeting place until he founded a community of the White Brotherhood, calling it 'Sunrise' ('Izgrev') by which time he was already in his sixties. From the outset, however, this brotherhood operated in small groups, coming together for rituals and for a shared meal (consciously or unconsciously emulating the Cathars, who in turn took their example from the early church). In the London Lodge right now we have a fine model before us as we make what I believe is a new start, beginning with a temporary home for the whole group to meet, which is in the Friends' Meeting House in Westminster (oh, and the founder of the Friends, George Fox, was a wandering preacher, too!).

These Westminster meetings are our 'shared meal' (maybe we will be able to expand on the idea) but the core of the London Lodge work will go on in people's homes: in healing groups,

*Liss, Hants. (White Eagle Publishing Trust) fourth edition, 2010, and second edition, 2015, respectively

in little discussions, in meditations, and so on. I'd like to suggest that they offer a real pattern which goes right back through all the examples I have given to the beginning: the small group, which meets on the basis of love one for another, but which links with another group, and another, and another, into one great honeycomb: a pattern I wrote about in the August *Stella Polaris*.* Are we just a little closer to the early Church, to the Cathars, even to the Polaires, who were at their best when a little group of five or six only?

Small but equal, respectful always of one another's spirituality: this may yet turn out to be the model for the Aquarian age. Close enough to love one another, few enough to support each other, united enough to offer our love and our service to each other little group in an overarching Lodge and to the greater whole. And to life on all levels.

When Spirit chooses, we shall have a new London Lodge. I long for that moment – but meanwhile let's pick up on the Cathar example and make the most of being, just for now, 'on the run'.

*I.e., in 'The White Eagle Cathar: 6'

Christmas Gifts

The White Eagle Cathar: 8 (December 2014)

THIS IS the second Christmas to pass since I began this series of articles, and maybe it will be time soon to move on. Before I do, here are some more thoughts about Christmas from a Cathar perspective. I pointed out last Christmas how Cathars were aware – in a similar way to White Eagle – of the dual nature of Jesus: the little human babe, born in a stable, to earthly parents, and the one so much greater, whom White Eagle calls 'the Christ' to distinguish him, the being who enables us to see the possibility of true spirit life and how it can be embodied. I have argued here that what is special about the Cathars' belief is how they established a real sense of living the true spirit life on earth, by virtue of the extraordinary responsibility held by the *parfait*, that of actually living the life of Christ. And in imitation of the Cathars, the birth that we seek through our work in the Lodge is to bring about, collectively, that elusive 'standard of life which is harmony with the infinite love', a phrase so often quoted in our documents.

So I find myself wondering, through the message of Christmas and the message of the Cathars, how can we best bring about that extraordinary achievement? First, I suppose, we should turn to the message Christmas brings above all: the innocence of the little child. It is a gift of the imagination, partly: the eyes of the tiny child whom we see in pram or on shoulder speak so easily to us of our home above, which the baby has so recently left. The simple gifts we exchange are messages of love, just as they were when the Magi brought them to Jesus. They are messages of respect, too, respect for the Christ within every one whom we bless with our gift or even just honour with a card.

'The light in me salutes the light in you' is the perfect message of those gifts, and if they are humble gifts, so much the more so. We remember at Christmas that truth is essentially simple, and that in White Eagle's message as in all religions, it comes down to just two things:

to act with kindness and to be grateful, which is the same as to be mindful.

Simplicity is so deeply the message of Christmas, that many of us, I think, shudder at the complexity materiality places upon it. White Eagle actually helps us to enjoy the fun: I find myself sometimes much less able than he seems to be to rise above the depression London's Oxford Street sets off in me as the Christmas shopping season approaches its peak. Materialism is depressing; in the scheme of things it is actually meant to be, I believe, until we redeem it by seeing the light in all of it and thus 'redeem' it. And that is distinctly Cathar too, in my understanding. But to work from simple mindfulness, from gratitude for each moment, is the best way to overcome the towers of material wealth that have so little of care lodged in them.

Care, yes. The Cathar *parfait* was mindful of the duty of care, always. His or her most important task was to be with the dying, to make sure that their material death was a birth into spiritual light. That normally meant administering the *consolamentum*, if the dying one was ready. If it is beautiful to look into the eyes of one just born

it is also beautiful, I think, to look into the eyes
of one dying, and many readers will have heard
me speak of how the light in the whole of my
mother's countenance as she lay dying convinced
me that she was most consciously 'walking into
the light' as she passed. Maybe for those facing
their first Christmas after a bereavement to think
of death as birth will itself by comforting; it certainly is for me, three years after Ylana died.

I have written of how the *parfaits* travelled not
just from château to château but from simple
home to simple home. Every home they went to
was, in its own way, a stable or a cave. Legend has
it that Cathars used caves as places of initiation. I
am not quite sure how well founded the legend
is, but I am certainly convinced that the symbolism of a cave is right for initiation. We go right
into the darkness, sometimes, for something to
be born in us. Christmas is a symbol of facing
the darkness, facing the loss of the physical sun,
reminding ourselves of its endless continuation
and coming through into a greater light.

I think I am right in saying that the tradition of a Christmas crib, a re-enactment in clay,
wood or (today) plastic figures of all those who

traditionally stood around the newborn Jesus in his cave or stable, goes back to Francis of Assisi. Francis was an almost exactly contemporary of the Cathars, and there is an intriguing possibility that his father was exposed to Cathar thought in northern Italy, while his mother came from roughly the Cathar area of southern France. It's far too much of an assumption to think of the Christmas crib as Cathar, but contemplation of this simple creation at the least takes us back to the uncomplex devotion of the mediaeval mind.

How lovely it would be if we could also show that in the Cathar one of the symbols that most resonated was the Star of Bethlehem? Sadly our scant records of them do not include this symbol as far as I know, and yet I am sure we rightly connect ourselves in the Lodge with them as a manifestation of the same brotherhood as our own. Dear Cathars, we are with you at this time, we who hold the responsibility now that you held once! Our enemies, the agents of materialism, are not so different from the ones you faced. You saw them in a powerful church, and in greedy nobles who swept down on you from the northern lands. Our greedy nobles are there, too: our powerful church is the church of consumerism, and our message is just the same as yours. Be simple; be kind; be non-violent to all, including the animals; love all, however different their perspective from our own; let the material world have no hold on us. And in this new age, let us be non-violent to ourselves too: see the little child within our own hearts, and bring our gifts to that too. Happy Christmas!

Catharism without Boundaries

The White Eagle Cathar: 9 (February 2015)

THERE'S an intriguing theory that sees the line of Cathar ancestry not in the traditional way via the Bulgarian Bogomils and round the northern Mediterranean over many centuries, but instead via the southern Mediterranean, and it runs like this. First, you have to take up the very attractive idea that one of the ways in which Cathar beliefs were carried from place to place, and in particular from château to château, was by virtue of the troubadour minstrels who passed though, with their own intriguingly mystical and potentially codified lyrics and rhymes. The troubadours, it is argued, offered an idealization of the feminine which was the basis of the ideal of courtly love. The Cathar respect for the feminine, marked out as unusual, then might arise alongside. Romantic legends, such as that of Esclarmonde de Foix, Cathar heroine, obviously fit well with this.

The troubadour theory becomes considerably more intriguing if we take another risk and agree with a theory that is well supported but not proven, which is that the origin of the troubadours lies in Islamic Spain, called by the Moorish invaders *Al-Andalus*. In short, the basis for it is Andalusian love-poetry, which can switch easily from the erotic to the most sophisticated evaluation of the feminine, at will. What is particularly exciting for us about this theory is that the culture we are talking about was largely that of the Sufis, the Islamic mystics. Neoplatonic elements are also noted in the Andalusian songs.

The twentieth-century Sufi writer Idries Shah reflects a connection forward from his own culture when he says, in his book THE SUFIS, that Catharism is saturated with Sufi thought. Frustratingly, he gives no evidence of this.* But we do know that the Sufi poets, whom modern western readers now find so attractive, certainly deal with an idealized and spiritualized concept of love, which encompasses in a continuum the erotic and the sublime.

*THE SUFIS (New York NY, Doubleday, 1964)

Our Cathars gain a radiance from such links as these. What were their own views about gender, love and sex? On the first, one thing we know is that they viewed the sexes equally; I've just had cause to go through sixty or so names of those known to have gone to the stake at Montségur, and there is every evidence of this in that list. On love, in the courtly sense, we know little except by taking up the troubadour connection. But on sex it's widely, and to a point correctly, assumed by visitors to the Languedoc that they were against procreation; the commitment made by the candidate or appellant receiving the *consolamentum* involved full abstinence from the sexual act – and the injunction to go out in pairs underlined the sense that your commitment was there for scrutiny. Many committed to Cathar devotion later in life! In contrast, White Eagle actually encourages us to enjoy the gifts that God has given us, all of them – and so presumably including sexual union, so the Cathars may come across to us as both strict and sombre.

Readers will know that I am not sure that such a view is really fair. To bring another soul down into an earthly body was to tie it into the slavery of being human, certainly, but since humans had a task, the reclamation of the heavenly state, I suppose it was always possible to argue that incarnated souls were needed. My reading – a personal one – is that though commitments were absolute, Cathar teachers were admonishing rather than punitive in their guidance, up to the time a commitment was made.

If procreation was the issue, then what about sex that was not likely to result in birth? It is perhaps unsurprising that alongside all the other things they were accused of, the classic charge of sexual deviance was levelled at Cathars and heretics who preceded them. It's an old trick. There is at least a tiny bit of logic in the accusation, for once: homosexuality at least did not carry the same risk of bringing souls into the world that heterosexuality did. However, I know of no evidence that same-sex union was actually thought well of, only that it was a popular accusation against Cathari.

White Eagle is quite interesting on so-called 'moral issues'. He points out how much morality differs from culture to culture, both geographically and through time, and rather dissociates himself from the constructs that are conceived by human beings:

'Every time the soul does not live truth from its innermost being, it is sinning. Sin is not of the body only – indeed, the bodily sins we would not call sins at all. Sin is the failure of the soul to live truly.' (THE PATH OF THE SOUL, chapter II)

I have strayed, however, from my topic of a tradition moving across the southern shores of the Mediterranean. We now need to be very sketchy, more even than we have been already. The hint of Neoplatonism I've mentioned would take us mainly to Egypt; thence we would have to look round to the eastern shore, and so to the Holy Land itself. Ephesus and the young church established by John would be even further around, beyond the Lebanon and into Turkey.

So the trail is at best incomplete. It is interesting primarily because what White Eagle people may be looking for, beneath all the historical talk, is evidence of a continuous, though frequently hidden, brotherhood. Mention of the Sufis helps us enormously in that – a brotherhood tradition in its own way unbroken for a thousand years and more. But there is another reason to be interested in looking at Cathar roots this way round. It helps to explain the open-hearted embrace Cathars are said to have offered both Muslims and local Jews. We tend to forget that their neighbours in Spain were Moorish; more locally, the university at Montpellier, famous in the history of medicine, was rich with both Arab and Jewish students and teachers. If the general theory of this article holds water, then the Cathar/troubadour culture might also have fostered the development of learning. It had, at least, broken free from the priestly hold, and had its own vernacular gospels.

St John has been ever-present in the background in these articles, and there is a final topic I'd like to introduce for next time. By way of introduction, here are some of the words by which White Eagle himself takes us into the fourteenth chapter of St John's gospel.

'It is not wise to try to understand this profound yet simple chapter with the intellect alone; only with the development of the inner light will the meaning become clear. Only through a spirituality which is lived and expressed through warm and kindly human relationships ... can the soul understand the profundity of Christ's teaching.'*

This fourteenth chapter is the one of 'In my father's house are many mansions' (v. 14), a phrase often taken to be supportive of reincarnation. Right now it feels to me, and with great warmth and happiness, that what is meant by those 'mansions' is a state of consciousness such as it how it feels to be part of this Lodge, or part of the brotherhood of the Cathars. The mansions are, as White Eagle calls them in THE LIVING WORD OF ST JOHN (p. 133), 'resting-places'. So what was it like to be in the 'resting-place' provided by the Cathar fraternity? In our next, and final, article we shall be looking at the ritual of the consolamentum.

*THE LIVING WORD OF ST JOHN, 4th edition, p. 133

The Consolamentum

The White Eagle Cathar: 10 (*April 2015*)

THIS SERIES of articles ends with a look at the most famous, and most mysterious, practice associated with the Cathars, the giving of the *consolamentum*. It is said that the *consolamentum* was the final initiation, that it took those who went through it into a place beyond the wheel of rebirth. It made men and women Christlike, in principle; it gave to them the words of Jesus to transmit and to exemplify among all human beings, beginning with the Lord's Prayer. It gave them power to console. It allowed them to pass from this world to the next in peace and in contentment. It saw them, figuratively or literally, through the flames.

Yet when we look at the words of the ceremony – for they exist, preserved (with what irony!) by the Inquisition – seven hundred years on, they surprise us with their orthodoxy. Three manuscripts contain them, one in Latin (now in Florence) and two in Provençal (at Dublin and Lyon). Of the last of these the writer Walter Birks informs us: 'In this liturgy of Lyon, written in the Langue d'Oc of the twelfth century, we recover the very atmosphere of the first centuries of Christianity in Asia Minor and Syria, down to the very wording in some cases'.* It is not entirely clear how he can make this bold statement, but as he was in Syria for much of the Second World War on intelligence work and found himself within a community that had apparently preserved rituals concerned with the Holy Grail from a very early period, amidst and hiding within an Islamic tradition, I am inclined to trust him. In short, were the Christianity of St John in Ephesus to have continued into the days of the Cathars, these *consolamentum* words may be the most representative we have; rituals are arguably the most lasting aspects of tradition. There is also the possibility that when details were fed to the Inquisition, crucial moments were carefully omitted – though the three manuscripts are quite similar in what they share.

*THE TREASURE OF MONTSÉGUR, p. 98

The words we have begin with a rite known as the *apparelhamentum* or *servitium*, a kind of general confession. There then follows the *melioramentum*, which is an adoration of those who, already classed as *parfaits*, are understood to exhibit the Christlike qualities, and a prayer in turn that all present may avoid 'an unworthy death' and be led to 'a good end' (that is, themselves receive the *consolamentum*). What follows, the *consolamentum* proper, is also described as the *traditio*, the 'formula of tradition', which suggests antiquity. Except in the case of the *consolamentum* for the dying, it would only have been offered to candidates (appellants) who had been through a period of training, the *abstinentia*. It was introduced by biblical references to authenticate its doctrine, among them the famous words from the fourteenth chapter of St John, '*If ye love me keep my commandments. And I will pray the Father, and He shall give you another Comforter, that He may abide with you forever*' (v. 16).

Then, with much repetition of the prayer itself, the process of giving to the appellant the power of speaking the Lord's Prayer begins. This is the key to what is being transmitted, but the words also stress the connection with the words of St John the Baptist in St John's gospel, 'And I knew him not: but he that sent me to baptize with water, the same said unto me, Upon whom thou shalt see the Spirit descending, and remaining on him, the same is he which baptizeth with the Holy Ghost.' (1 : 33). All around are lights, candles and such, to emphasize the holy fire, but the actual transmission is by the laying on of hands while the candidate comes forward in a series of genuflections.

Before the actual transmission can take place, the appellant has promised solemnly to obey the rules laid down for him which include semi-vegetarian diet, absolute non-violence, sexual abstinence, and travelling in pairs like the very first Apostles (Luke 10).

The laying on of hands is authenticated by Mark (16:18): 'They shall lay hands on the sick and they shall recover'. In effect this ceremony, which is completed by the administration of a kiss of peace and the cloaking of the candidate, is performed in full recognition of more words from St John: 'These things that I do shall ye do also, and greater than these shall ye do' (14 : 12). In short, fully to come into the service of Christ is to be endowed

with all those things with which Christ is endowed, potentially. In this awareness, but humble under the dark cloak known as the *sadere*, he
or she walks forth from the ceremony.

Hearing of this service only by manner of
its words, the reader might quite reasonably feel
puzzlement that such a ceremony could have so
profound an effect. The answer must lie, I suspect, in the words of White Eagle that I quoted
last time, 'Only through a spirituality which is
lived and expressed through warm and kindly
human relationships ... can the soul understand
the profundity of Christ's teaching'.* When the
whole ceremony is acted out, the heart opens
much faster than when the words are read upon
the printed page. We feel it almost as much in
our bodies as our minds: those that enact it, I
have found, contain a form of muscle memory
that both enables and ennobles the imagination.
The whole enactment is much, much more
profound than the mere the words indicate.

By the end, something has happened which
is hinted at in the service when the words, '*And
He shall give you another Comforter*', are used. The

*THE LIVING WORD OF ST JOHN, 4th edition, p. 133

idea of comfort, consolation, is quite implicit in the title of this ceremony. What does it mean? John 14 is quite clear that the Comforter is 'the Holy Ghost' (v. 26), '*Even the Spirit of truth: whom the world cannot receive, because it seeth him not*' (v. 17). But White Eagle is clearer still.

'What is this Holy Ghost? Who is the Holy Ghost? We can only endeavour to convey the idea in the following words: The Holy Ghost is the holy breath, the in-breathing of wisdom and of love. By the way you live, if you follow the example of Jesus, there will come to you this baptism, this in-breathing of the Holy Ghost: this is the initiation of the divine fire, the divine wisdom within. If it has lived the life as taught by Christ, when the soul turns to inward contemplation and meditation, the Holy Ghost enters it, and the holy breath or presence is felt, indescribably in words and which only the initiate knows and can understand. The Holy Ghost is a manifestation of the divine fire, the divine magic.'*

The Holy Ghost also takes form in the gospels as the Dove, carrying a message from above such as '*This is my beloved Son, in whom I am well pleased*' (Mat-

*THE LIVING WORD OF ST JOHN, 4th edition, p. 135

thew 3 : 17). As the doctrine of the Trinity took shape, it became the third person of the same.

I have said on many occasions before, so will only briefly do so now, that I have the strongest possible sense that at the moment my beloved mother Ylana, called by White Eagle 'Christian' after a different pilgrim, passed on, she moved rejoicing into flames that consumed all of her 'that was of the earth, earthy' (a White Eagle phrase). It is this joy that is so significant in the Cathar. It is the sense of having come through something, having given up all, and yet absolutely and most visibly having been welcomed into the world of light, in full consciousness. Everything is given up, and yet everything is won.

Epilogue

WHAT CAN we learn from people who lived lives very different from our own, over seven hundred years ago? There are plenty of lessons for our individual lives, if we choose to listen to them, but I will best leave the reader to glean from the foregoing chapters, lest I seem to make moral exhortations. The impression that above all remains with most of us is of people who had such a certain – but inclusive – belief system that even death had no power over them.

What I think is less obvious is the communal example that the Cathar model offers us. Where today is such great dignity and mutual respect held by individuals in a group for one another? Where is there such discipline, offered quite voluntarily? – for the Cathars offer us no hierarchical models, no chain of command, no sanctions beyond an agreed assumption that to break the commitment you had made was to start all over again on the path. Cathars needed to demonstrate nothing by the size of their movement; as far as we know, their unit was the small group or brotherhood, and although there may have been some seniority within it, that is a long way from the outcome of hierarchy. From such a group came, too, what today we would call non-violence; a more Cathar word might be harmlessness. *Absolute* harmlessness, though the rule was broken once or twice. We look right ahead to Gandhi before we find another such example.

Neither do we find, in the Cathars, a morality that set up a system of one person being better or worse than another. The striving to attain perfection, in the Cathar sense, is not something that involves comparisons with others – in part, because the requirement of commitment in a *parfait* was absolute. Cathars seemed to have had personal goals, not peer evaluation. Which among us could find ourselves able to commit in the way they did? I wonder.

Your purpose is to establish on the earth plane a way of life which is in harmony with the infinite love.

I've also tried, in this book, to stress the sense for me, at least, of how strongly the Cathars stand in the tradition of St John. I have a kind of interest in pursuing this, because of my grandmother's vision in which St John featured so strongly. I was reminded recently how it was a second visionary experience that featured St John, in meditation in Italy in 1966, that led to the building of the White Eagle temple in Hampshire in 1974. I too have had a strong personal contact with John, in a meditation at Lordat which I recounted in a chapter in the book THE VIEW, of a smiling, young figure looking at me, and I wrote: 'The smile I saw absolutely radiated love, but a love that was not for me only but for all humankind'.* The vision came back to me strongly on seeing a particular painting at Questhaven (see p. 11).

This book highlights a contrast between an idealistic vision, held by some (not many) today and maybe by only a few seven or eight hundred years ago, with what sceptics will call 'the reality', the strife of the marketplace, as it were. I think that is a narrow term. Yet in speaking of Cathars themselves we are dealing with mediae-

*See pp. 44 and 57–8 of THE VIEW: FROM CONAN DOYLE TO CONVERSATIONS WITH GOD, edited by Dave Patrick. London, Polair Publishing, 2009.

val people, and there are plenty of examples, in the historical books about them, books derived mainly from Inquisition records, of individuals who took their commitment lightly. The most famous reincarnation memories, too (the ones told to Arthur Guirdham, see p. 10), certainly describe fallibility in the main, and scarcely more men and women of ideals than the Inquisition records afford us. We cannot know, truly, what it was to be a Cathar or if indeed there were any who truly reached the goals I believe them to have set themselves. Any who did have remained anonymous, at the least. All we know is that the ideals were strong enough for them to hold together, and to die together without protest, for to them it was not life that mattered most, but the triumph of the light.

Appendix I

1. The Dance of Jesus
(See above, p. 48)

'We would not have you limit your saints to your Christian church. There are many, many saints all over the world, unattached to any organization or organized religion. They are saints because the love in them causes them to give selfless service to life, to other creatures and to other people. Saints because the joy of heaven bubbles in them and they want to sing and dance. You may or may not remember the hymn and the dance of Jesus. It is not in your orthodox version. You will find it in the Apocrypha, when Jesus danced with joy and sang with joy, the joy of the spirit, the joy that he felt in the Father–Mother God.' (White Eagle Inner Teaching)

2. The Age-Old Ceremony of Christmas
(See above, p. 55)

'The ceremony of the rebirth of the light is as old as creation, as old as life itself on this earth, and the ancient brotherhood is still there, still enacting a grand cosmic ceremony year by year. The brethren participating in it are invisible now; there are human brethren and angelic brethren. If you were able to open your vision to the scene at Christmas time (the winter solstice) when the actual birth of the Christ child is enacted, you would see the most beautiful movement, hear the sound and rhythm of the music of the heavens, and hear the great paean of praise, hear the very creative power and Word which is being used. You would hear the chanting of the great AUM, the inbreathing and outbreathing, the invoking of the spirit to bless and bring something holy, good and pure to the earth with the rebirth of the light.'

Excerpt from the Inner Teaching, 'The Dual Meaning of the Sun Child's Birth', in *Stella Polaris* (Vol. 63, no. 1, December 2013)

3. Affirming Community
(See above, p. 60)

The text on p. 60 speaks of London White Eagle Lodge members finding that 'their community is a bonding one with another around shared belief, and is not tied to the building [they] are leaving'. The following words are a compilation from little slips of paper upon which members of the community described what the

London Lodge meant to them. There were four groups reporting.

1. 'We come together in a safe place – a spiritual family – with memories of 'the old school' but moving from discipline to finding the essence of sacredness and sanctity. A place of opportunity, to be with others, to be still, to put into service White Eagle teachings that reach the heart. A place to be alone with the peace that can be found if we look. A family feeling, and a place to replenish the soul. We are true brothers and sisters here in the Lodge.'

2. 'Community of purpose: we're like-minded people. Respect, non-judgmental atmosphere with diversity and tolerance. Brotherhood. Loving support and safety. A sense of peace within the community. Mindfulness. A shared sense of humour. The opportunity to give service, including healing. The knowledge that our voices are heard.

'We gain greater freedom to be. Uplifting of spirit and contact with the higher self. A better chance of being a better person. The opportunity to be still. The love, compassion and patience we find.'

3. 'Like-minded, but different – the diversity of our community. Living with imperfection: you don't have to be perfect to come here. People are authentic. It's an environment of trust. A place to iron out personal difficulties, to pare down the demands of the ego. You can't have the rose of spiritual Heart without thorns. A place where people are of goodwill.

'The place is an enigma, the purpose of which you only understand by surrender. A community that has faith in the power of Spirit and our own ability to access this. Constant learning. A spiral path where one meets the same lessons, but at different levels. The perennial questions have the same answers. A place where something very precious is looked after with great sensitivity.

'Friendship; healing is also very strong. The adaptability of the community to move into a post-hierarchical experience. Here is somewhere we give brotherhood a chance.'

4. 'Peace: companionship, friendship, harmony – qualities you feel when here and take away with you. It's multilayered. Deep calling. Love that binds together and creates: a place for people to come and receive healing and where the commitment to serving helps us all grow.

'There is a label attached to the work here: a newcomer can feel it is a place based on a particular teaching. Yet no feeling of having to give up one's cherished beliefs. The community is genuine in trying to explore that 'standard of life which is in harmony with the infinite love'. The value of an open community which is inclusive and has aims such as that 'standard'. The peace and welcome you are given as an outsider, coming in.

'We allow people to BE, because all people have gifts.'

From a feature in *Stella Polaris*
(Vol. 63, no. 2, February–March 2014)

4. The White Dove
(See above, p. 76)

Scientists feel that there must be laws that control the invisible worlds around you. They do not understand them yet, and we dare to say that when the scientist and the spiritual person on earth meet and agree there will be a tremendous step forward upon the path of humanity's spiritual evolution – the Comforter, the Comforter symbolized by that white dove which has been seen so many times.

When you imagine you have seen a beautiful white bird, remember that imagination is the creative gift of the spirit. All that you have on your earth that is built or created is the result of an idea which has come to a man or woman from the plane of idea, the plane of creative power. That idea has touched and been received by a certain part of the physical brain, a part that is there for the purpose of being a receiving station. This has yet to be discovered by the earthly scientists. Doctors will learn in time the use of certain areas in the brain; they are already beginning to get a glimpse of the possibilities which are in the mind, brain – we say soul and heart.

The white dove that comes into your midst, and which you see through your imagination, symbolizes the Comforter. It is the impression of truth, the messenger which conveys to a person wisdom and knowledge of the kingdom of heaven both after death and before death. When a person has seen and heard this messenger he or she does not need any kind of material or scientific proof.

This is why we are here to help you: to train you to reach that transcendental consciousness, not to raise you from the earth and its practical demands, but to strengthen you in your daily life and to give you the wisdom to live your life to its very fullest. We would train you to live your life not only for yourself, but for God and in the service of God, which means of course co-operation with the ancient law of Brotherhood. Remember that all the Great Ones have achieved their greatness through their life, through individuality, through their training in a body, a form.

From a teaching in *Stella Polaris*
(Vol. 63, no. 4, June–July 2014)

Lightning Source UK Ltd.
Milton Keynes UK
UKOW02f2120260215

246908UK00001B/1/P